Wonderful Water

Rosie Hankin

Illustrated by
Stuart Trotter

Evans

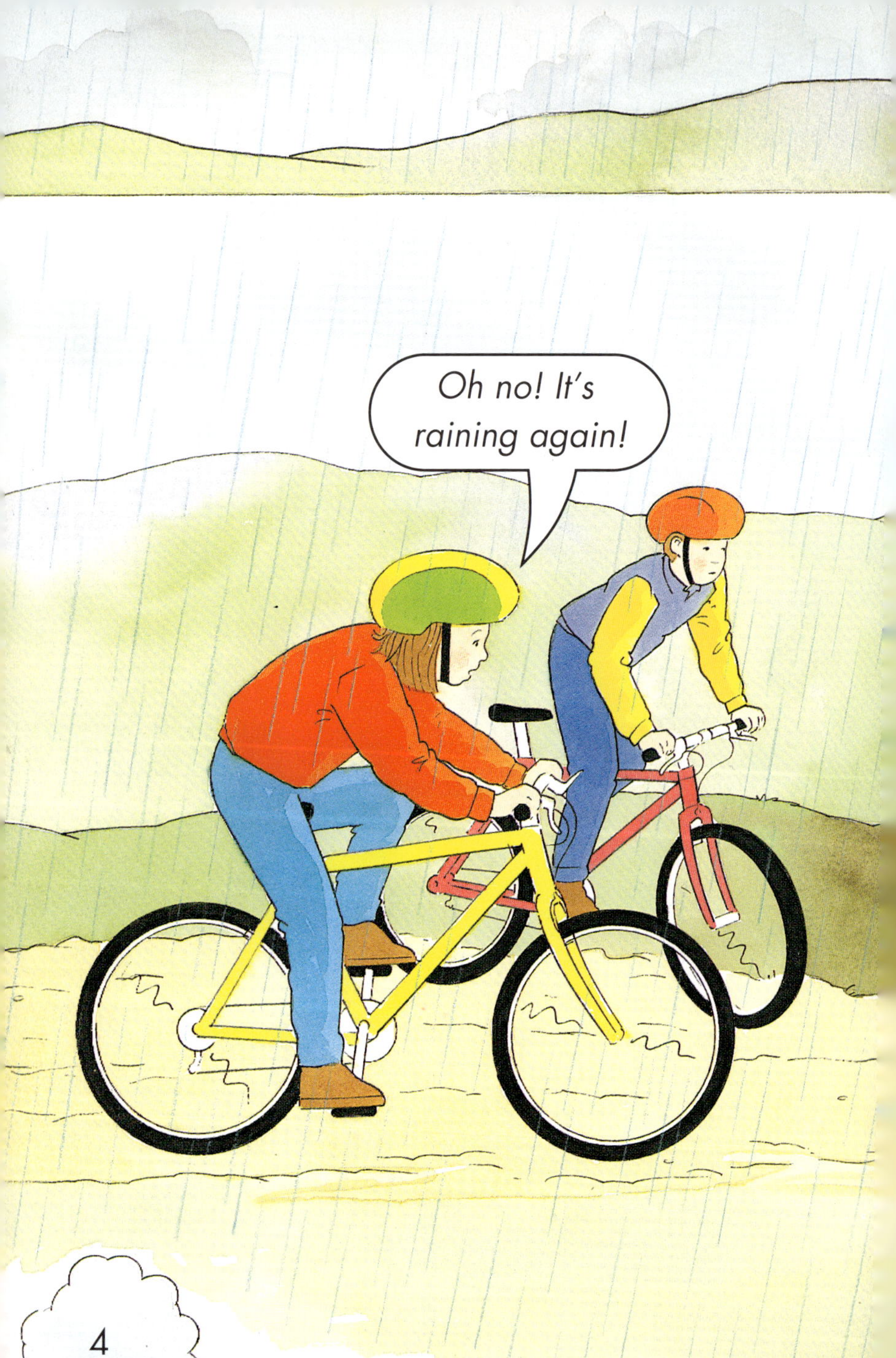
Oh no! It's raining again!

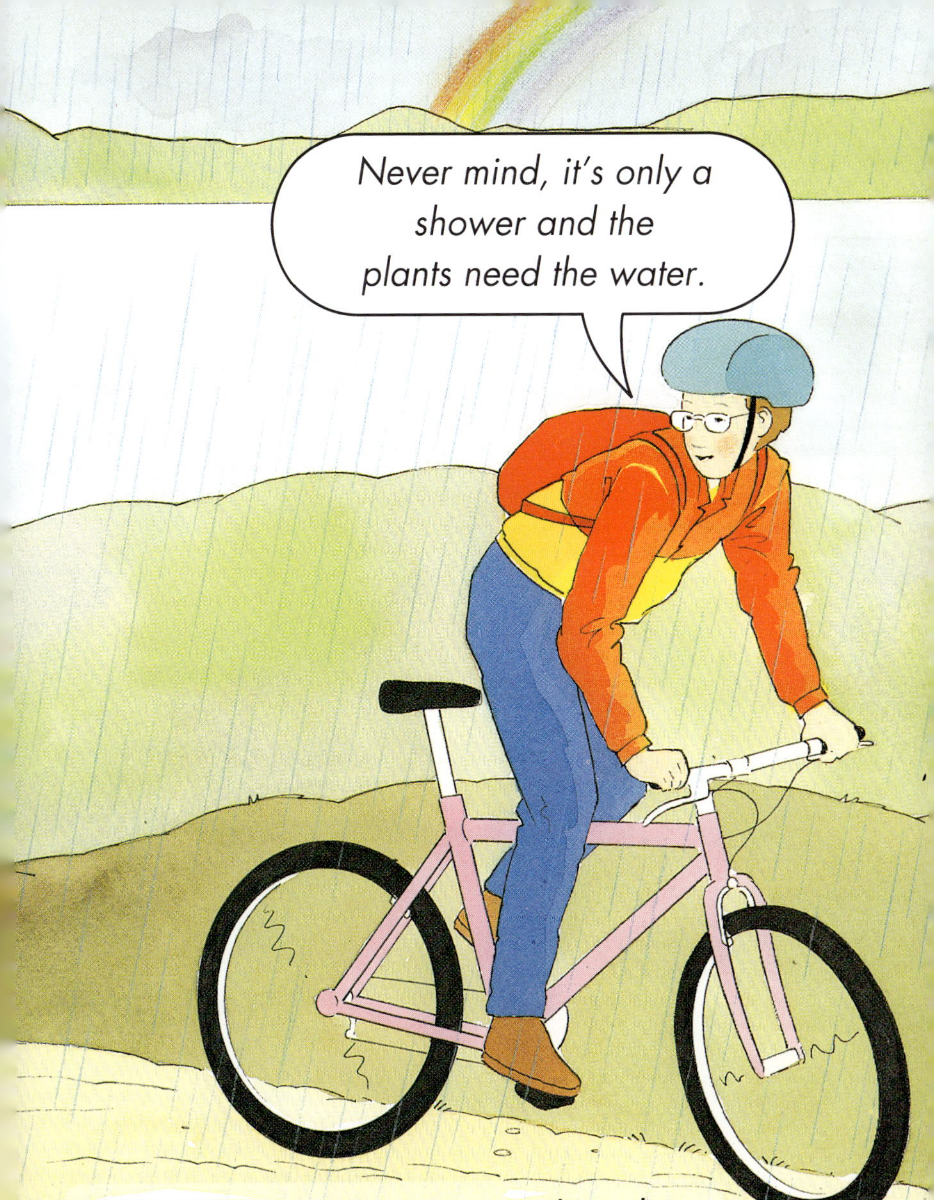

All plants need water so that they can grow.

The sheep don't seem to like the rain.

Some of them are sheltering under the tree.

If there is too little rain the grass will not grow. Then there will not be enough grass for animals, such as cows and sheep, to eat. All animals need water to drink, too.

Where does all this rain-water go?
Some of it soaks into the ground and some joins the streams that flow down the hill.
Let's cycle down the track following the stream.

The rainfall is higher in hilly areas. Some of this rain-water falls into streams and this makes the streams flow very fast.

The small streams then join other bigger streams and become rivers.

Look at the boats on that huge lake!

That's not a lake, it's a reservoir.

10

A reservoir is a place where water is collected. Then the water is pumped out to be used for other things.

A dam controls the amount of water that flows out of the reservoir. There are huge gates under the water which are opened and closed depending on how much water is needed.

13

14

Water from the reservoir is cleaned by passing through a filtration plant. This removes all the mud and germs. Then the clean water is pumped to houses and factories.

Water tower

16

There are huge machines inside a hydroelectric power station called turbines. Water that flows from the reservoir spins the turbines to make electricity.

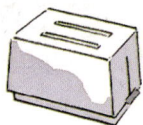

So the rain-water helps to give us electricity?

18

We make water work for us to make our lives more comfortable.

The river is much smaller down here.
Look at the animal tracks in the mud.

Deer, foxes and birds come to the river to drink. They, too, need water to survive.

I'm hot. I need a drink of cold water.

When we are hot our skin sweats. We need to drink to replace the water we have lost as sweat.

Just think, this water was once raindrops!

It probably came from the reservoir.

24

We use water in our homes all the time for washing, cooking and for flushing the toilet.

Where does the water go when it runs out of the sink?

Or when we flush the toilet?

Dirty water flows along pipes to a sewage plant.

26

At the sewage plant water is cleaned and purified. Then the clean water is pumped back to houses and factories.

Water is pretty amazing stuff!

28

I think it's wonderful!

All living things need water to survive. But people use water in all sorts of other ways too. We use it in swimming pools, in baths and for cooking.

We use it to work for us to make electricity. We all use lots of water every day.

Can you use these pictures to remember the different ways that water is used?